Book 1

Your First Guitar Method

Mary Thompson

Chester Music

(A division of Music Sales Limited)

8/9 Frith Street, London W1V 5TZ

About your first guitar book

This book will help you to learn the guitar in very easy stages. In Book 1 you will find out the names of the notes, and how they are written down, as well as some of the signs and symbols used in music.

Practise the tune on each page until you can play it without any mistakes, before going on to the next page. When you can play all the tunes in this book, you are ready to move on to Book 2.

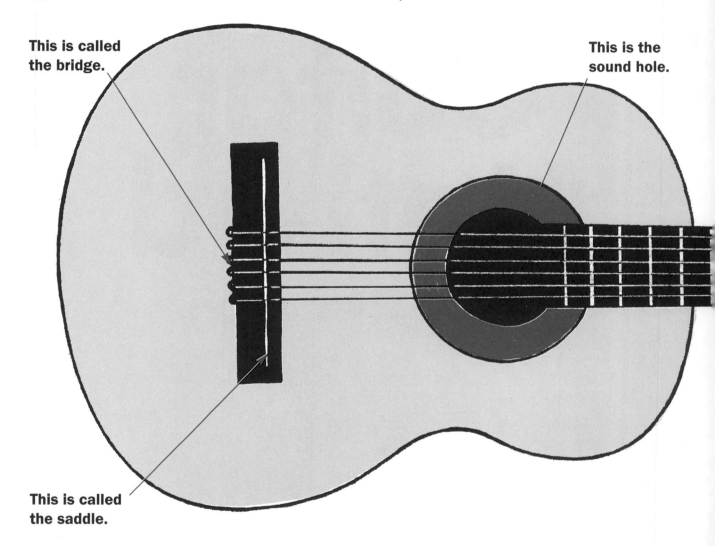

This is called the bridge.

This is the sound hole.

This is called the saddle.

This book © Copyright 1999 Chester Music.
Order No. CH61568   ISBN 0-7119-7577-9

Music and text setting by Mary Thompson
Illustrations by Nigel Hooper
Cover design by Ian Butterworth
Printed in the United Kingdom by Printwise (Haverhill) Limited, Haverhill, Suffolk.

About your guitar

Below you can see what all the different parts of your guitar are called. You make a sound by gently plucking the strings with your right-hand fingers and thumb, or with a small piece of plastic called a plectrum.

Each string has a name. You can see the names of the strings below. The sixth string sounds the lowest and the first string sounds the highest. Pluck some of the strings and listen to the sound they make.

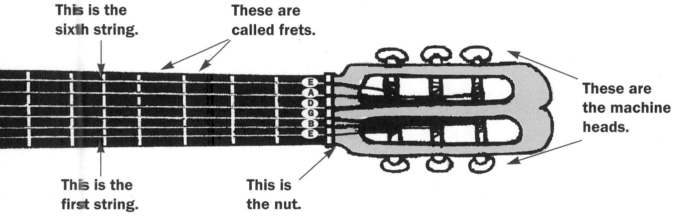

This is the sixth string.

These are called frets.

These are the machine heads.

This is the first string.

This is the nut.

Tuning your guitar

How high or low a string sounds is called its pitch. Before you start to play, you need to make sure all the pitches are correct. This is called tuning. There are several ways to tune your guitar strings.

You can buy pitch pipes from most music shops. Blow one pipe at a time, and turn the machine head for that string until the pitch sounds the same.

If you have a keyboard, you can tune the strings to this. Below you can see which key to press for each string.

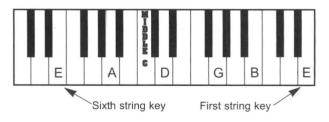

Sixth string key   First string key

On an electronic tuner, a dial tells you when each string is the correct pitch.

How music is written down

Music is written on a set of lines, called a stave (or staff). In guitar music, there is a sign called a treble clef at the beginning of each stave.

This is a treble clef.

This is a stave.

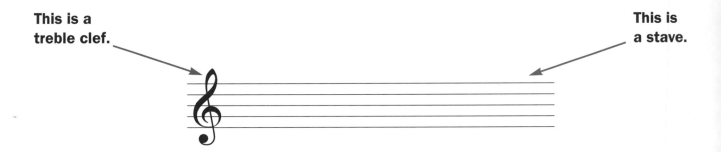

Another way of writing guitar music

There is another way of writing guitar music, called tablature. Tablature has six lines, each one representing a guitar string.

You can find out how to read tablature below. In this book the tunes are written on tablature as well as the stave.

This is what tablature looks like.

This tells you to press one of your left-hand fingers down, at the first fret of the first string. Press down just to the left of the fret.

This line represents the first string.

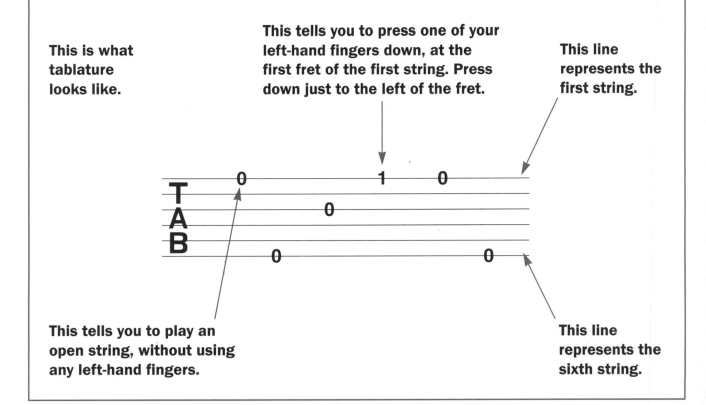

This tells you to play an open string, without using any left-hand fingers.

This line represents the sixth string.

Musical notes

When you write a story you use words to make up a sentence. In music, you use notes to make up a tune.

Notes are named after the first seven letters of the alphabet, from A to G. The higher a note is on the stave, the higher it sounds.

You can see the names of the notes below.

Some notes go on the lines.

Others go in the spaces between the lines.

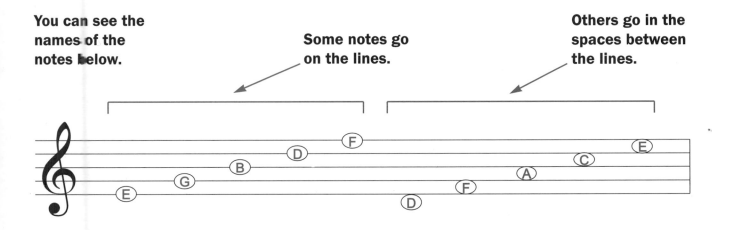

Remembering the names of the notes

To help you remember the names of the notes, you could make up some funny phrases. Here are some examples.

Why not try making up some of your own? You could use the names of people you know.

For the notes on the lines:

Every Great Big Dragon Flies

For the notes in the spaces:

Don't Forget Auntie Catches Everything

How long notes last

Notes can last for different lengths. The length of a note is measured in steady counts, called beats. You have to count the number of beats very carefully as you play. On the right you can see what a semibreve looks like. Semibreves are also called whole notes. A semibreve lasts for four beats.

Every time you play a semibreve, you need to count to four before playing the next note.

Splitting music up into sections

When you write a story you leave a space between each word. This makes it easier to read. Music is split up into short sections too. Each section is called a bar. The bars are separated by lines, called bar-lines.

At the beginning of the music there are numbers to tell you how many beats are in each bar. These numbers are called the time signature. Always look at the time signature before you start to play.

This is a time signature.

This time signature tells you there are four beats in each bar.

This is a bar-line.

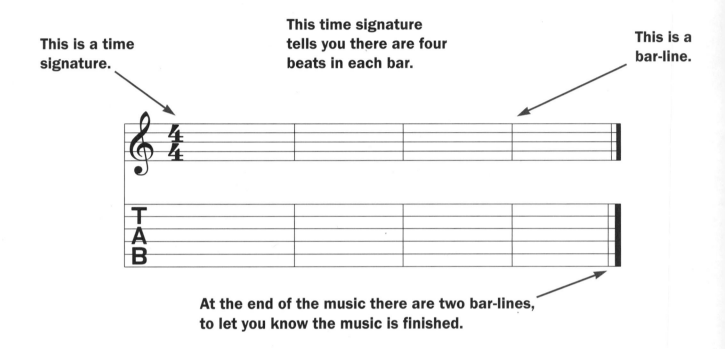

At the end of the music there are two bar-lines, to let you know the music is finished.

How to sit

If you have a classical guitar, rest the curved part on your left thigh. It helps to have your left leg raised slightly, either by crossing your legs, or by using a foot-stool. Hold the neck of the guitar a bit higher than the body.

If you have an electric guitar you might find it more comfortable to rest it on your right thigh, depending on its shape. The most important thing is that you are sitting in a relaxed and comfortable position.

Using your left hand

Rest your thumb on the back of the neck between the first and second frets. Then arch your hand so that your fingers are over the strings, keeping your fingertips upright.

When you press a string, press it just to the left of a fret. If the sound is fuzzy, you need to press harder on the string. Make sure your nails are quite short.

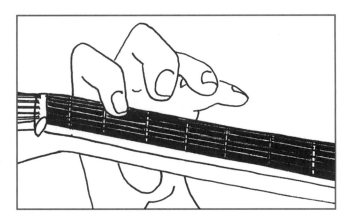

Using your right hand

If you want to use a plectrum, hold it between your thumb and the side of your first finger, between the first joint and the tip. Use the pointed end to strike the strings.

You can find out about using your fingers and thumb in Book 2, but for now, use your first finger to pluck the strings if you are not using a plectrum.

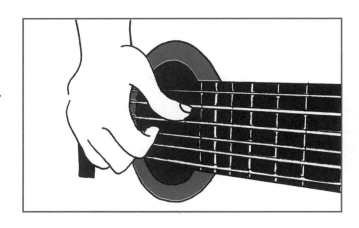

Your first note

The first note you are going to learn is E. Here you can see where to find E on your guitar, and how it is written on the stave. Try playing E a few times on your guitar.

This is where E is written on the stave.

This is the nut.

This means play an open string.

This is the first fret.

This is the first string.

This is the sixth string.

The first string is E.

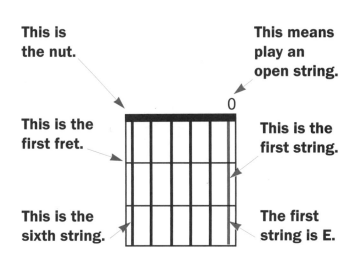

A different note-length

On page 5 you learned about semibreves. On this page you will learn about notes which last for two beats, called minims.

If the time signature at the beginning of the music is 4/4, then you can fit two minims in each bar.

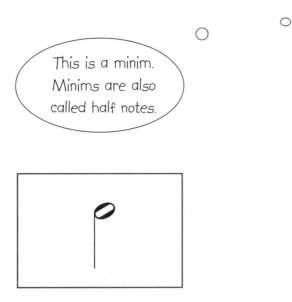

This is a minim. Minims are also called half notes.

Easy E

Here is a tune to help you practise playing E. Strike the string with a plectrum, or the first finger of your right hand, then count to two before striking it again.

Try to count as evenly as you can.

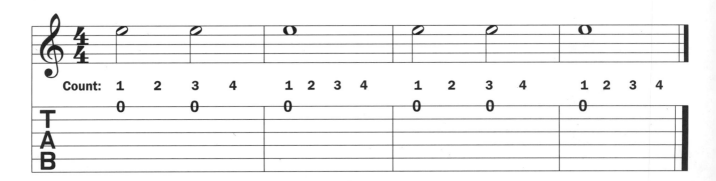

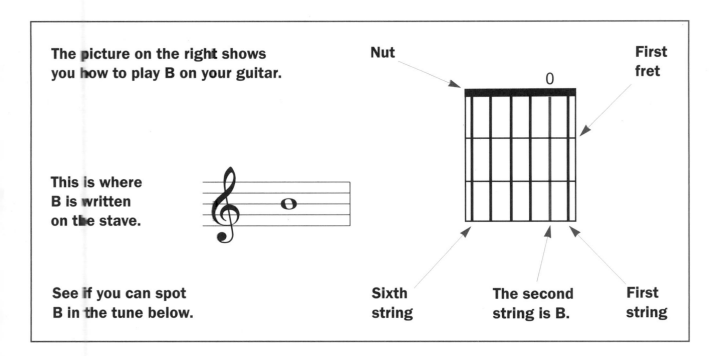

The picture on the right shows you how to play B on your guitar.

This is where B is written on the stave.

See if you can spot B in the tune below.

Nut

First fret

0

Sixth string

The second string is B.

First string

Two's Company

Remember, count two beats when you play a minim and count four beats when you play a semibreve.

Try to count the beats in your head if you can.

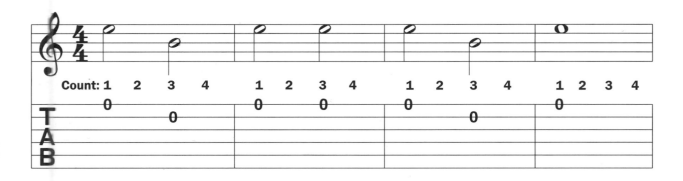

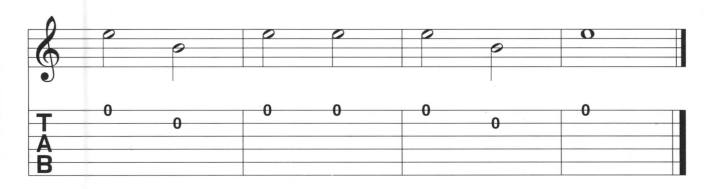

Another note-length

So far you have learned about semibreves and minims. On this page you will learn about crotchets, which last for one beat.

If the time signature at the beginning of the music is 4/4, then there are four crotchets in each bar.

This is a crotchet. Crotchets are also called quarter notes.

Crazy Crotchets

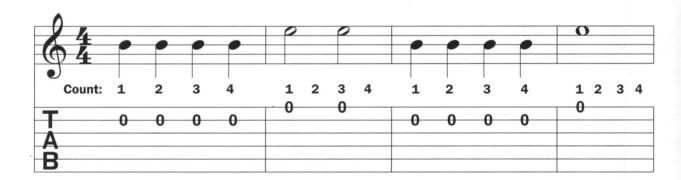

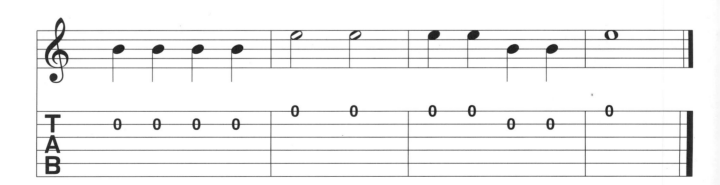

The picture on the right shows you how to play D on your guitar.

Sixth string | Nut | First string

This is where D is written on the stave.

Press down just to the left of this fret, using your third finger.

Look out for D in the tune below.

Third fret | Second string

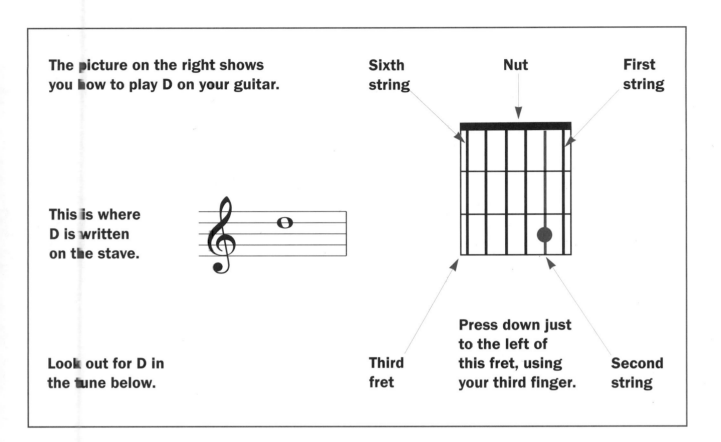

Daydreaming

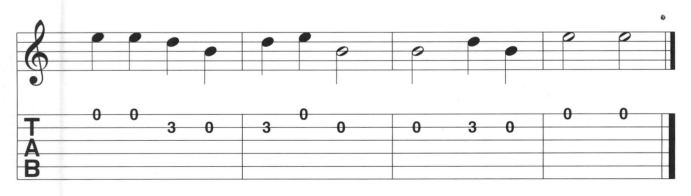

Count: 1 2 3 4 1 2 3 4 1 2 3 4 1 2 3 4

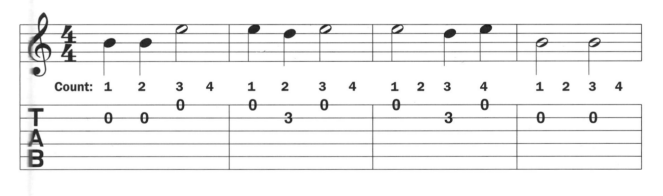

More about your left hand

When you play notes using the frets, you need to think about which fingers to use. Use your first finger for the first fret, your second finger for the second fret, and so on.

In the tune below, remember to use your third finger to play D.

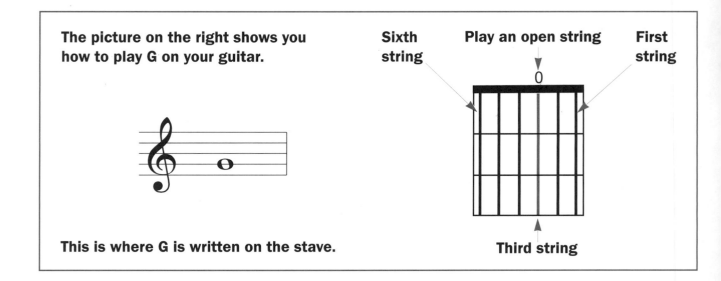

The picture on the right shows you how to play G on your guitar.

Sixth string

Play an open string

First string

This is where G is written on the stave.

Third string

Gee Whiz!

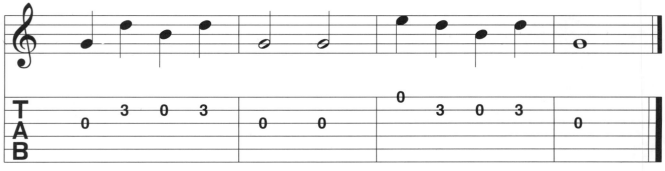

A new time signature

There is a new time signature in the next tune. It has a number three on top instead of a number four. This means there are three beats in each bar.

Triple Trouble Waltz

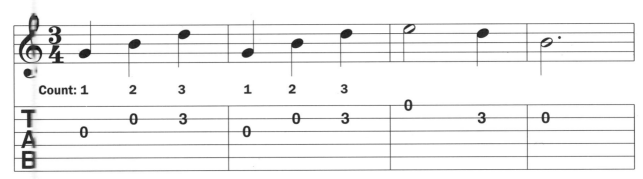

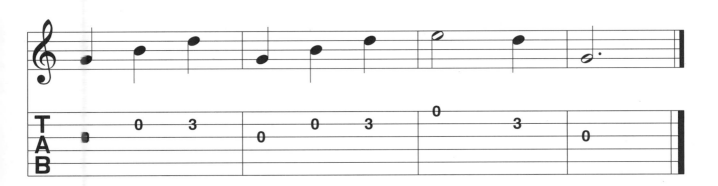

Practice hints

- Before you start to play, make sure your arms and fingers are very relaxed.

- Start by playing something you can already play well, to help give you confidence.

- Practise for a few minutes each day, rather than for a long time once a week.

- When you play something new, try to play it all the way through, even if you make some mistakes.

Repeat signs

There is a new sign at the end of the tune below. It is called a repeat sign. When you see this sign, go back to the beginning and play the music again. The second time you reach the repeat sign, stop playing.

Practise "Over And Over" slowly at first, until you are sure of the notes. Then try playing it faster, bit by bit. This is a good tune to start your practice with, because it relaxes the muscles in your fingers.

Remember to play the music again whenever you *see* this sign.

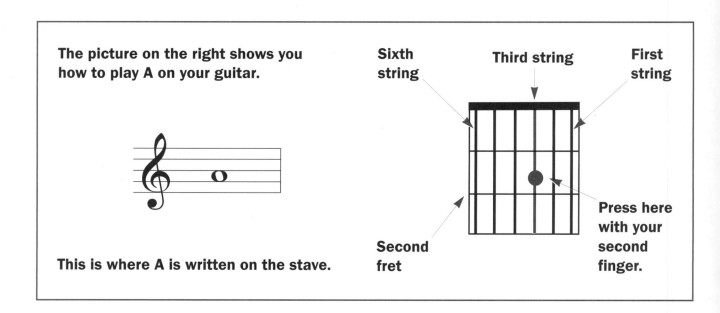

The picture on the right shows you how to play A on your guitar.

This is where A is written on the stave.

Sixth string

Third string

First string

Second fret

Press here with your second finger.

Over And Over

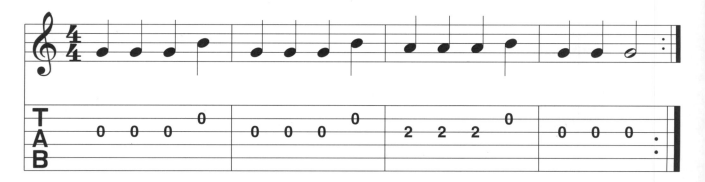

When you see the word piano, or the letter p, play the music quietly.

Playing quietly

There are words in music to tell you how loudly or quietly to play. These words are in Italian, because the first printed music came from Italy. The Italian word for "quietly" is *piano*, sometimes shortened to *p*.

To play notes quietly, strike the strings very gently. Try playing a few notes. Strike the strings hard for some, and gently for others. Notice how loud or quiet each note sounds.

Lullaby

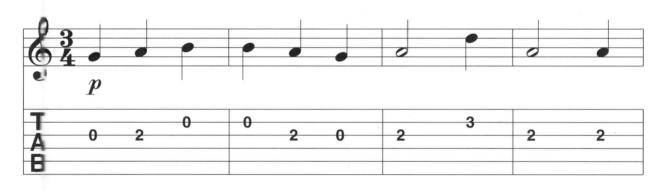

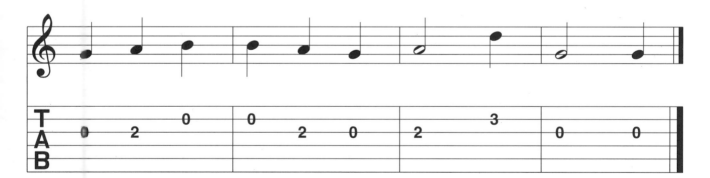

Practice hints

- Choose a time to practise when you are not likely to be disturbed. It will be easier to concentrate.

- If you feel tired, stop playing. You will learn far more if you are feeling fresh and alert.

Music Quiz

On this page there are some questions about the things you have learned so far.

The answers are all in this book, so you can check to see how many you get right.

1 How many beats do you count for this note?

2 What is the letter-name of this note?

3 Which left-hand finger do you use for this note?

4 What is the letter-name of this note?

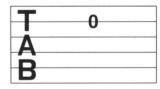

5 What is the Italian word for "quietly"?

6 How many bars are there in this tune?

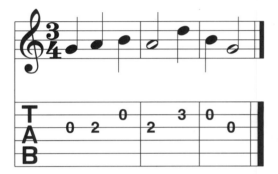

7 If the time signature is 3/4, how many beats are there in each bar?

8 What does this sign mean?

9 How many beats do you count for this note?

10 What does the letter *p* mean in music?

Now you are ready to move on to Book 2!

Your First Guitar Method

Mary Thompson

About Book 2

Following on from Book 1 in the series, this book will help you to develop your guitar skills one step at a time. In Book 1 you learned the names of the notes, and some of the signs and symbols used in music. In Book 2 you will learn more guitar techniques, and begin to play more than one note at a time.

Here are some reminders of the things you learned in Book 1. See how many you can remember.

This is a minim, or half note. It lasts for two beats.

This is a treble clef.

This is a crotchet, or quarter note. It lasts for one beat.

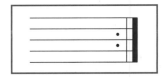

This tells you the music is written in tablature.

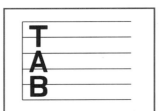

This is a time signature.

This is a repeat sign.

This is a semibreve, or whole note. It lasts for four beats.

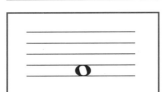

_P_ is short for _piano_. It means "play quietly".

Notes you have learned so far

Here is a reminder of all the notes you
learned in Book 1.

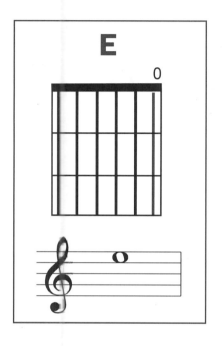

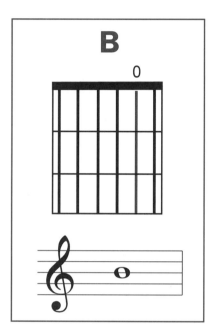

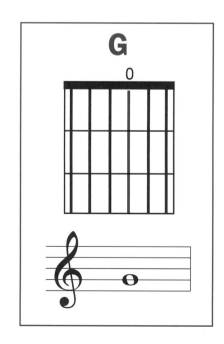

Playing loudly

In Book 1 you learned the Italian word *piano*, which means "quietly". Sometimes you have to play the music loudly. The Italian word for "loudly" is *forte*. The word *forte* is often shortened to *f*.

To play loudly, strike the strings harder, keeping your fingers a little more upright. Try playing a few notes, striking the strings harder for some. Listen to how loud or quiet each note sounds.

The picture on the right shows you how to play another D on your guitar.

This is where D is written on the stave.

See if you can spot this D in the next tune.

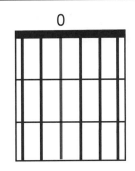

This D sounds lower than the D you learned in Book 1. Play both Ds. Can you hear the difference?

Shout It Out

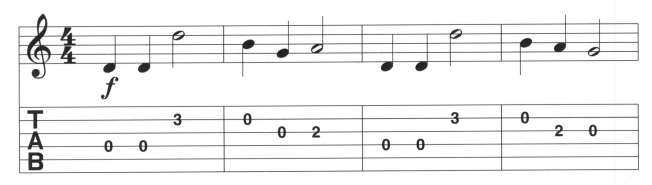

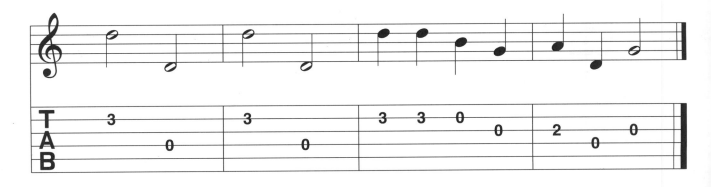

20

The picture on the right shows you how to play C on your guitar.

This is where C is written on the stave.

See if you can spot this C in the next tune.

In the tune below, remember to play C using the first finger of your left hand.

By The Sea

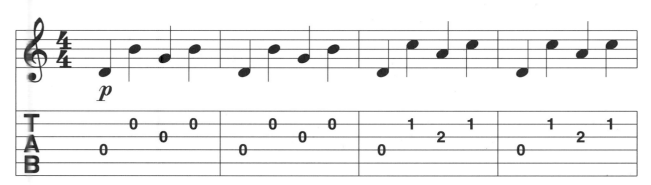

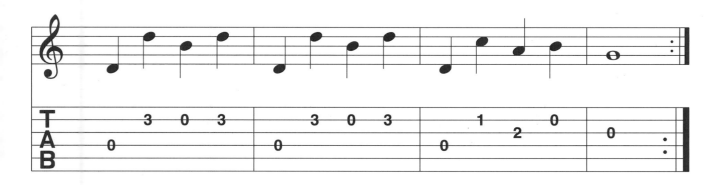

Remember to play "By The Sea" quietly.

Dotted notes

Sometimes there is a dot after a note. This makes the note last for one and a half times its normal length. For example, a minim lasts for two beats, so a minim with a dot after it lasts for three beats. When there is a dot after a note, it is called a dotted note.

This is a dotted minim. Dotted minims are also called dotted half notes.

Polka Dot Waltz

Remember to play this tune loudly.

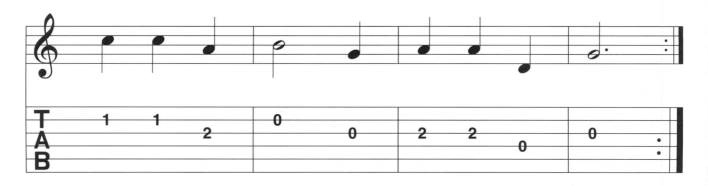

22

Leaving gaps in music

There are signs in music that tell you to leave gaps. These gaps are called rests. When you see a rest, count the correct number of beats in your head, before playing the next note.

A crotchet (or quarter) rest = 1 beat ❳

A minim (or half) rest = 2 beats ▬

A semibreve (or whole) rest = 4 beats ▭

A semibreve rest is also used to show a rest which lasts for a whole bar.

Take A Break

To stop the strings from sounding during a rest, gently touch the strings with the side of your right hand. This is called damping the sound.

You can practise counting this rhythm by clapping the beats. Miss one clap for a crotchet rest and two claps for a minim rest.

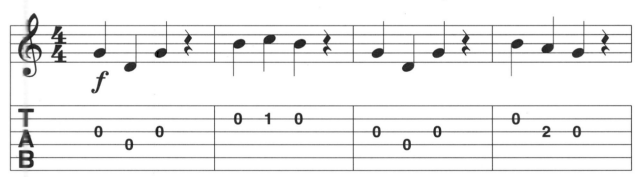

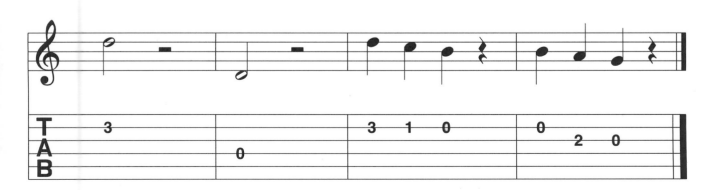

Using your right-hand fingers

In Book 1 you learned to pluck the strings with your right-hand first finger, or a plectrum. As you learn to play more notes, you need to start using your first three fingers and thumb. This helps to make the music sound smooth. Use your thumb to play the bottom three strings and your fingers to play the top three strings.

Your right-hand fingers and thumb have special names in guitar music. These names are in Spanish. Usually they are shortened to the first letter of each word: p, i, m and a. You can see which letter goes with each finger on the right. You do not need to use your little finger in this book.

'P' stands for pulgar, which means "thumb"; 'i' stands for indicio, which means "index finger"; 'm' stands for medio, which means "middle finger", and 'a' stands for anular which means "ring finger".

Right On

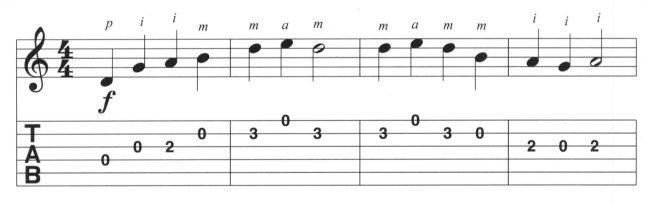

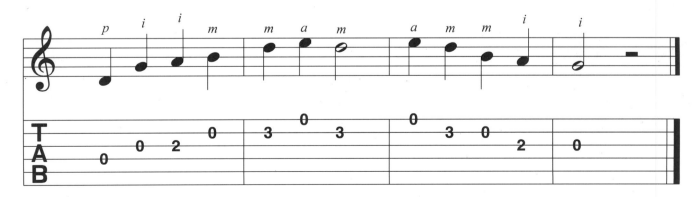

Using your left-hand fingers

When you are pressing a string with a left-hand finger, you do not always have to remove it straight away. Sometimes it is better to keep pressing it down until you need to remove it.

For example, in the tune below, you can keep your left-hand fingers down for the whole of the first two bars, and the fourth and fifth bars. This is much easier than removing them after each note.

The picture on the right shows you how to play F sharp on your guitar.

This is where F sharp is written on the stave.

A sharp sign in front of a note makes it slightly higher. The sharp sign also applies to any other Fs later in the same bar.

In the tune below, all the Fs are F sharps. Press down with the second finger of your left hand.

Stay Sharp

Remember, this note is F sharp too.

Playing two notes at the same time

So far you have only played one note at a time. Now you will start playing two notes together. Don't worry if you find it a bit difficult at first. The more you practise, the easier it will become. There are some tips below to help you.

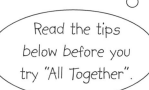

Read the tips below before you try "All Together".

All Together

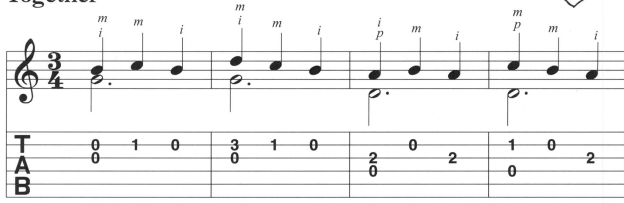

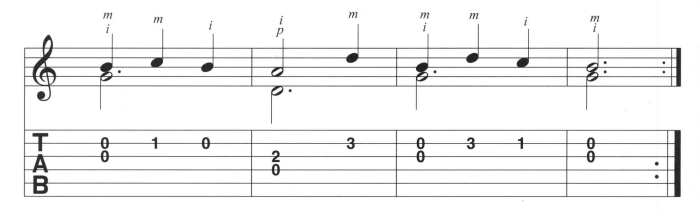

Practice hints

- Remember to use the correct fingers for each note.

- Try to pluck both strings at exactly the same time.

- Start off very slowly at first. When you are sure of the notes, gradually play the music faster until you are playing at a comfortable speed.

Another note-length

Here you are going to learn about a shorter note, called a quaver. A quaver lasts for half a crotchet beat. It looks like a crotchet with a tail.

Quavers are often joined together in groups of two or four. This makes them easier to read. You can see what they look like below.

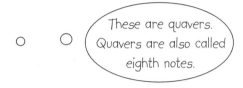

These are quavers. Quavers are also called eighth notes.

This is how two quavers are joined together.	

This is how four quavers are joined together.	

Quivering Quavers

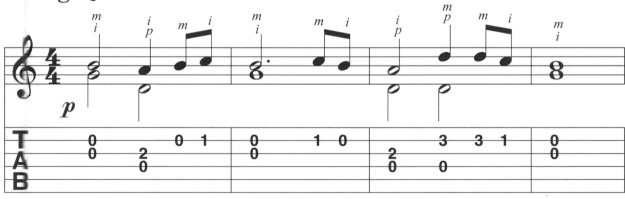

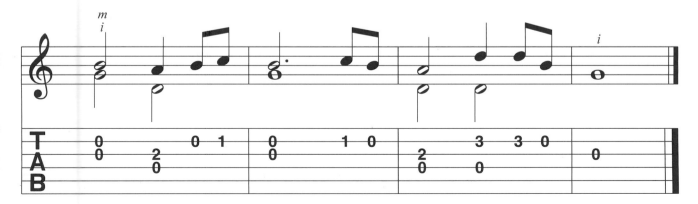

Dotted crotchets

A dotted crotchet lasts for one and a half crotchet beats. You can see what a dotted crotchet looks like on the right. To play dotted crotchets, it helps to count "one and two and". Before you play the next tune, try clapping the rhythm.

This is a dotted crotchet. Dotted crotchets are also called dotted half notes.

The picture on the right shows you how to play another A on your guitar.

This is where A is written on the stave.

This A sounds lower than the A you learned in Book 1. Play both As and listen to the difference.

Can you spot both As in the next tune?

Medieval Magic

28

The picture on the right shows you
how to play another G on your guitar.

This is where
G is written
on the stave.

Can you spot both Gs in the next tune?

This G sounds higher than
the G you learned in Book 1.

Merry-go-round

Playing chords

Groups of two or more notes played at the same time are called chords. In guitar music, chords are often used to accompany melodies, especially in songs.

The chord you are going to learn here is called a D major chord. The name of the chord is often written as a letter above the music, instead of writing out all the notes.

The picture on the right shows you how to play a D major chord.

This is where the notes are written on the stave.

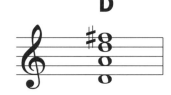 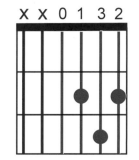

An x tells you not to play that string.

The numbers tell you which left-hand fingers to use.

Press down at the frets, as shown above, then play each string on its own to make sure you can hear all the notes clearly.

When you can hear all the notes clearly, run your right-hand thumb, or a plectrum, across the strings.

Major Player

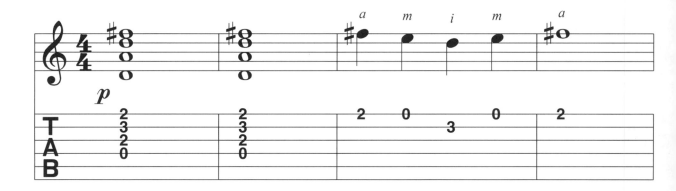

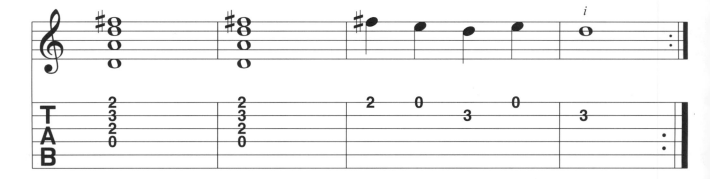

Tied notes

Sometimes the same notes are joined together by a curved line, called a tie. When notes are joined together like this, you add the number of beats together and play one long note. For example, if you see a semibreve tied to a minim, you play one note lasting for six beats.

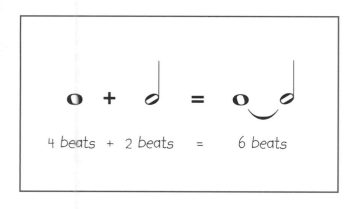

All Tied Up

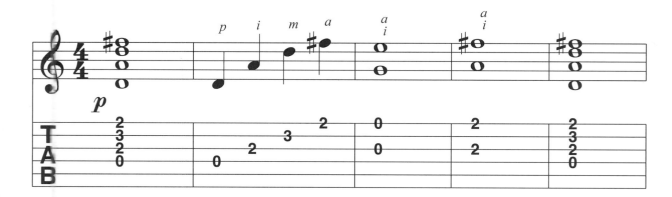

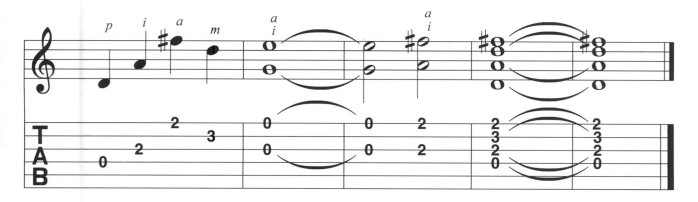

Congratulations!

Now that you have reached the end of the book, here is a special piece for you play. Practise it until you can play it all the way through without any mistakes. Then you can play it to a friend or relative, to show them what you have learned.

Farewell

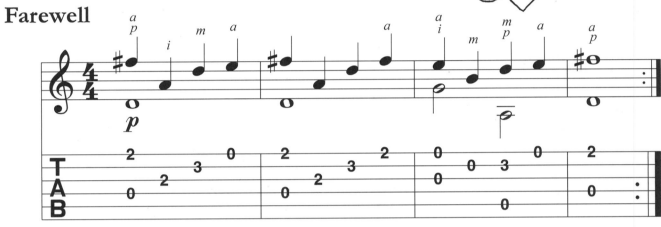

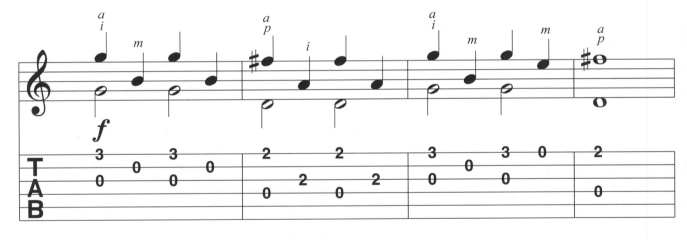